BUILDING LINKS BETWEEN FUNDING AND QUALITY IN HIGHER EDUCATION

India's Challenge

LINDSAY DAUGHERTY | TREY MILLER
RAFIQ DOSSANI | MEGAN CLIFFORD

This research was funded jointly by RAND's Center for Asia Pacific Policy (CAPP) and RAND Education and was supported in part by the generosity of RAND's donors and by the fees earned on client-funded research.

Library of Congress Control Number: 2013944749

ISBN: 978-08330-8123-0

The RAND Corporation is a nonprofit institution that helps improve policy and decisionmaking through research and analysis. RAND's publications do not necessarily reflect the opinions of its research clients and sponsors.

Support RAND—make a tax-deductible charitable contribution at www.rand.org/giving/contribute.html

RAND® is a registered trademark

Cover design by Pete Soriano

© Copyright 2013 RAND Corporation

RAND OFFICES

SANTA MONICA, CA • WASHINGTON, DC

PITTSBURGH, PA • NEW ORLEANS, LA • JACKSON, MS • BOSTON, MA

DOHA, QA • CAMBRIDGE, UK • BRUSSELS, BE

www.rand.org

Preface

In December 2012, India released its 12th Five-Year Plan (FYP), which will determine India's planned spending on development across government sectors through 2017. The FYP describes a number of challenges facing India's higher education system, including rapidly expanding demand for higher education, widely varying quality among institutions, and unequal access to higher education for disadvantaged groups and regions. To address these concerns, the FYP calls for a paradigm shift in India's system for higher education governance, granting greater autonomy and accountability to institutions, and shifting from a "command and control" model to a "steer and evaluate" model. In addition, the FYP calls for an increase in funding for quality efforts to align funding with the new priorities for quality improvement.

One potential approach that has proven effective in other countries and may hold promise for India is to develop policies that explicitly link funding to well-defined quality measures and quality assurance processes. The FYP offers a number of reforms that are likely to improve quality, yet there is no discussion of explicit links between quality and funding. These ideas have occasionally been discussed among Indian policymakers, yet this approach has never been laid out in policy documents as a promising policy tool for improving higher education quality in India. In this report, we review the related research literature to describe how policies linking quality and funding are being used in other countries to improve the quality of higher education. We then present a vision for how policies linking funding and quality could be similarly adopted to strengthen India's higher education system. The report should be of interest to national and state policymakers in India, as well as heads of affiliating universities and institutions. It should also be of interest to policymakers in other countries facing challenges similar to India's and to the academic community interested in governance of higher education systems.

The project was funded jointly by RAND's Center for Asia Pacific Policy (CAPP) and RAND Education. CAPP's mission is to support work that addresses the most critical challenges facing the Asia-Pacific region. RAND Education supports research on a range of important policy issues in K–12 and postsecondary education. The authors bring expertise on a range of issues, from measurement of college quality, to postsecondary access and success, to governance of higher education. More information about RAND is available on its website: http://www.rand.org.

Contents

Figures and Table

Figures

Table

Summary

Rapid Growth of Indian Higher Education Leads to Concerns About Quality

The higher education system in India enrolls the second largest number of students in the world after China—nearly 22 million. In the past two decades, enrollment grew by 7.7 percent per annum and more than quadrupled. The number of institutions has grown even more rapidly, from fewer than 6,000 in 1990–1991 to more than 46,000 today, the most of any country in the world.

India's spending for higher education has increased at the same time; it now spends at rates similar to other developing and developed countries as a percentage of gross domestic product, yet the growth has not been sufficient to keep up with ballooning enrollment numbers, and private spending has continued to outpace public spending (FYP, 2012; UNESCO, 2007). The funding is also heavily skewed, with most spending going to a small number of "national" universities owned and managed by the Indian government while many state colleges are severely underfunded and most private colleges are left to fend for themselves (Agarwal, 2009).

The rapid growth of the higher education system in India has raised concerns about the quality of education offered by the nation's institutions. A number of reports document the decline in quality that has accompanied the rapid growth and the insufficient quality of the majority of institutions (Agarwal, 2009; FYP, 2012; University Grants Commission, 2012). From the perspective of the labor market, industry surveys find that many graduates are unemployable without substantial on-the-job training (NASSCOM, 2005; World Bank, 2008).

New Five-Year Plan Calls for Reforms in Higher Education

In December 2012, India released its 12th Five-Year Plan (FYP), the nation's key policy document for higher education (and other social services) through 2017. The 12th FYP suggests a range of reforms to higher education to change the role of the national government from "command and control" to "steer and evaluate," giving more autonomy and accountability to the states and to the higher education institutions themselves with the goal of improving quality.

The 12th FYP's reforms reflect the argument by many that issues related to governance are a driving factor for the system's quality problems (Agarwal, 2009; Altbach, 2009; FYP, 2012). The vast majority of institutions are part of an affiliating system, in which primarily lower-tier colleges are responsible for teaching students, and the large state-owned universities with which the colleges are affiliated are responsible for setting curricula, giving exams, and granting degrees. The affiliation system is characterized by standardization, with colleges given little autonomy over curriculum, staffing, and programs offered (Agarwal, 2009). The state- and institutional-level regulations and controls are supplemented by controls imposed from a still higher level, the national government and its regulatory arms. This has led to a collection of unclear and often contradictory policies and laws that have prevented the government from implementing cohesive reforms (Agarwal, 2009; Hill and Chalaux, 2011).

The movement toward greater autonomy and accountability for institutions is a worldwide phenomenon, with countries increasingly building systems that encourage institutions to self-regulate and take responsibility for improving quality rather than trying to ensure quality through tight control over funding and decisionmaking by the government. Higher education systems that are moving toward greater autonomy and accountability often look to financial incentives as an important tool to steer the system. By creating policies that explicitly link quality and funding, countries can encourage institutions to pursue innovative strategies for quality improvement and hold institutions accountable when they do not move toward the goals set by the government and other key stakeholders. These policies can take a variety of forms, such as explicit formulas that link outcome quality measures to funding rates, grants for innovation, and requirements that institutions meet minimal quality standards to receive per-student funding.

In an effort to explore India's possibilities in implementing policies that link funding to quality measures as a means of improving quality, RAND researchers reviewed the FYP and the research literature on other countries' reform efforts. This report summarizes our findings and suggests seven policy actions the Indian national government and other stakeholders can take to improve higher education by linking funding to quality. Some of the suggested actions can be accomplished in the near term, and others will take more time. This discussion is relevant to reformers in other countries as well, since it reflects lessons learned by governments and institutions worldwide that face a growing demand from potential students, limited resources, and an urgent need to produce quality graduates.

A Course of Action for Improving Higher Education in India by Linking Funding to Quality

The experiences of other countries offer some general guidance to the Indian national government and other stakeholders as they transition the higher education system from a "command and control" to a "steer and evaluate" model. First, goals and quality measures must be defined, agreed on, and communicated to all parties, along with other relevant data. The quality measures must apply to public and private institutions. Policies linking quality and funding are not sufficient to ensure a high-quality system; a range of other supports, such as developing quality faculty and strengthening quality assurance bodies, are necessary for policies linking quality and funding to be successful. The government must keep in mind other priorities in education, such as access, sustainability, alignment with the K–12 system, and the needs of employers. Finally, it will be important to remember that change of this magnitude takes time and that policies may need to be adjusted along the way.

The findings of the RAND study can be summarized in a suggested roadmap for linking funding to quality in India as a means to support the vision described in the 12th FYP:

1. **Continue the Process of Developing and Implementing a Robust Accreditation System for Indian Institutions.** Accreditation distinguishes schools that adhere to a set of standards. In January 2013, the University Grants Commission (UGC), which is the primary national regulator of higher education, made accreditation mandatory for institutions that it regulates.[1] This stands in contrast to the literature, which suggests that voluntary accreditation with ties to incentives is more effective in driving institutional buy-in and compliance. In addition to concerns about compliance, it is not clear that existing accreditation bodies have the capacity to accredit all institutions. Yet India's accreditation system could be modified to overcome these and other potential drawbacks. For example, it could include tiered standards that are tied to the institution's own mission statements, a focus on outcome measures rather than input measures, and maximum transparency to stakeholders. Policies that link financial incentives to accreditation can encourage institutions to seek accreditation voluntarily, making them more likely to engage in the process, provide accurate information, and move toward quality improvement (Salmi, 2009).

2. **Develop, Implement, and Publicize a Quantitative Data System to Measure Quality of Higher Education Institutions and Institute Policies for Continuous Improvement over Time.** A new, decentralized system will need clear metrics by which to assess quality and progress toward national goals and a data system for managing the quality data gathered. The first step is to engage stakeholders, including students, employers, government leaders, university administrators, and

---

[1] See http://www.ugc.ac.in/pdfnews/8541429_English.PDF, accessed May 22, 2013. UGC regulates all higher education institutions except technical institutions. The regulators for these institutions are expected to follow UGC's lead. See edu-leaders.com, 2013.

faculty, to define the unique goals of higher education in India and determine a set of indicators to fairly and accurately measure institutional contributions toward those goals (Miao, 2012). A challenge for the proposed National Commission of Higher Education and Research (NCHER) will be to create a set of quality measures that will be dynamic and change as data become available while still winning stakeholder acceptance. Such measures could include *input* measures, such as students' test scores and teacher-to-student ratios, and *outcome* and *value-added* measures, such as graduation rates and students' salaries in the workplace after graduation.[2]

3. **Gradually Phase In Other Methods to Link Funding to Quality Measures.** The literature suggests that tying funding to quality can be a powerful tool to steer and evaluate institutions in a decentralized governance system. India could start by tying funding to the national accreditation process, as described above. India could also fund institutions based on enrollment counts as opposed to cost recovery. As capacity at the institution and state levels develops over time and India expands its data system, India can transition some funding toward performance-based budgeting (providing data on performance to institutions and asking them to develop budgets with an eye on improving performance) or performance contracts (a commitment from institutions to fulfill a number of national objectives in exchange for access to additional funding). These flexible methods to align funding with institutional goals have proven effective in many contexts, and can be implemented with varying degrees of quantitative data. However, these methods can be expensive and administratively burdensome, as institutions must work directly with the government to determine goals and demonstrate progress. Over time, as India develops a robust education data system and a complete system of quality indi-

---

[2] The future of the NCHER is in question given substantial concerns about the limitations that may be placed on state power under a strengthened central quality assurance body (Goswami, 2012).

cators based primarily on outcomes, some funding can be put toward explicit performance-based funding—a system that allocates funding based on specific performance measures, such as students' degree completion, instead of allocating funding based entirely on enrollment.

4. **Continue Efforts to Develop and Implement a Student Financial Aid System and Gradually Tie Eligibility to Accreditation and Quality Measures.** The 12th FYP calls for financial aid as a means to extend access to higher education to underserved populations and areas of the country, and that is the primary purpose of student financial aid systems worldwide (FYP, 2012; Johnstone, 2006). Student loan systems can play a valuable role in linking funding to quality by tying an institution's eligibility to receive student loan funds to basic quality standards.

5. **Continue Efforts to Expand Funding Available for Competitive Research Grants to Individual Researchers.** The 12th FYP calls for "more investment and focused efforts to build a vibrant research culture and strengthen the research capacity of the country," and more access to individual research grants is proposed as a means to this end. Peer-reviewed research grants have been introduced and need to be widely extended to make most research grants competitive and open to both the public and private colleges, as is done in public and private organizations around the world. To increase the level of funding for the grants and align funding with the country's goals for higher education, the national government has established bodies such as the Science and Engineering Council of the Department of Science and Technology. The national priority-driven and peer-reviewed processes of such federally funded research bodies in the United States as the National Science Foundation and the National Institutes of Health offer powerful models.

6. **Develop a System to Provide Competitive Grants to States, Institutions, and Departments to Spur Innovation and Achieve Specific National and State Goals.** Competitive institution- or department-level grants give state and national

governments opportunities to direct funding to specific goals that may change over time or differ across regions. These grants could similarly be used to incentivize differentiation, collaboration, structural changes (e.g., merging of institutions), and a variety of other priorities that are mentioned in the 12th FYP.

7. **Provide Funding to States and Institutions to Build Capacity for Self-Governance in the New "Steer and Evaluate" Model.** Some countries undergoing similar transitions have developed explicit technical assistance programs to help institutions and states change governance structures. Other countries have had success with academic audits, whereby institutions are coached by government officials through the planning and budgeting process (Dill, 2000; Saint, Hartnett, and Strassner, 2003). In India, the World Bank has funded the Technical Education Quality Improvement Programme (TEQIP), which is designed to help technical institutions introduce governance structures that grant greater autonomy to institutions from state university systems on matters such as infrastructure and curriculum development.[3] If TEQIP is shown to be effective, it could serve as a template for nontechnical institutions and for widespread application to the private colleges as well. The specific approach for capacity building in India, if any, should be based on a clear needs assessment.

---

[3] See All India Council for Technical Education, 2012.

Acknowledgments

We are grateful to RAND's Center for Asia Pacific Policy and RAND Education for supporting this research. We would like to thank Darleen Opfer and Michael Lostumbo for their guidance and support. This report benefited from valuable feedback during the quality assurance process provided by Cathy Stasz, Rita Karam, and Pawan Agarwal. Krishna Kumar and Charles Goldman also provided valuable insight in the planning stages. Finally, we would like to acknowledge Shelley Wiseman. Her writing assistance played a critical role in shaping the final report.

Abbreviations

AHELO	The Assessment of Higher Education Learning Outcomes
AICTE	All India Council for Technical Education
CLA	Collegiate Learning Assessment
CAAP	Collegiate Assessment of Academic Progress
FYP	Five-Year Plan
NAAC	National Assessment and Accreditation Council
NCHER	National Commission of Higher Education and Research
OECD	Organisation for Economic Co-operation and Development
PISA	Program for International Student Assessment
QAA	Quality Assurance Agency
SMHRD	State Ministry of Human Resources Departments
TEQIP	Technical Education Quality Improvement Programme
UCG	University Grants Commission
UMHRD	Union Ministry of Human Resources Department

CHAPTER ONE

India's Current System of Higher Education

Rapid Expansion and Concerns About Quality

The higher education system in India enrolls the second largest number of students in the world (after China), with nearly 22 million enrollees. The past two decades have been characterized by growth of 7.7 percent per annum, with enrollment numbers more than quadrupling over two decades, and the gross enrollment ratio (GER)[1] increasing from 12.3 to 18.1 percent in just the past five years (Agarwal, 2009; FYP, 2012). The 12th Five-Year Plan (FYP) sets 25 percent GER as a goal for 2017, a target that would add ten million enrollees over the next five years (FYP, 2012), or an annualized growth rate of 7.8 percent. Hence, policymakers expect Indian higher education to continue to experience the same rapid growth through 2017 as in the recent past.

The number of higher education institutions has grown even more rapidly than enrollment, from fewer than 6,000 institutions in 1990–1991 to more than 46,000 today, the largest of any country in the world. Indian higher education institutions are, however, significantly smaller on average than colleges in China or the United States (Agarwal, 2009). Two trends have driven growth. First is the shift toward private provision—over 10,000 degree-granting private institutions were established over the past five years. They now represent 64 percent of all institutions and account for nearly 60 percent of enrollment (FYP, 2012). While private growth has exploded, public invest-

---

[1] The total enrollment in a specific level of education, regardless of age, expressed as a percentage of the population in the age group corresponding to that level of education.

ment in higher education grew relatively modestly in the decade leading up to the 11th FYP. A small subset of public institutions owned and managed by the national government (most public institutions are owned by the 28 state governments) have received substantial new investment for improvement and expansion since 2007.

The rapid expansion of India's higher education system has been accompanied by a concomitant increase in concerns about the quality of the nation's institutions. According to Béteille (2005), the growth has been unplanned and chaotic, characterized by inadequate facilities, outmoded teaching methods, and a lack of quality faculty. A number of official reports comment on the decline in quality (Agarwal, 2009; FYP, 2012; UGC, 2012). These reports highlight concerns about low graduation rates and scores, and poor employment opportunities and salaries after graduation. Reports from the National Assessment and Accreditation Council (NAAC) suggest that most institutions are of poor or average quality. The evidence of a quality decline among the public is largely based on perceptions, as well as independent surveys by media sources and industry associations.

From the perspective of the labor market, industry surveys find that many graduates are unemployable without significant on-the-job training (NASSCOM, 2005; World Bank, 2008).[2] One report found that only 15 percent of general education graduates and 25 to 30 percent of technical education graduates are qualified for employment (NASSCOM-McKinsey, 2005). Graduates are weak not only in knowledge and skill formation but also in soft skills, such as the ability to communicate well in the workplace (Hill and Chalaux, 2011).

The concerns about quality are particularly strong for private colleges and some of the state universities. The highest-performing students (often those who are relatively advantaged) attend a few prestigious public institutions that are directly regulated and generously funded by the national government. The vast majority of students are enrolled in lower-tier public universities and private colleges. The latter vary widely in quality and tend to be of lower quality than most public

---

[2]   The issues with graduate employability stem from both the overall low quality of institutions and a mismatch between the programs offered and the skills needed in the workplace.

institutions (Sunder, 2010). Private colleges have been more adaptable in course offerings and are typically commercially oriented (Levy, 2006). Yet they are typically perceived to be of lower quality than public institutions and cater to students who have the capability to pay tuition but cannot gain entry to more selective colleges (Carnoy and Dossani, 2012; Levy, 2006). State universities suffer from underfunding and overregulation, resulting in poor infrastructure, difficulty hiring quality faculty, unwieldy affiliating systems, and little opportunity to innovate or improve (Agarwal, 2009). Even the national institutions—those of the highest perceived quality—are not able to compete with internationally renowned universities. There is not a single Indian university among the top 200 in the Times Higher Education rankings or the Academic Ranking of World Universities (FYP, 2012).

Governance

Many, including the national government itself, argue that the relatively poor quality of India's higher education sector stems primarily from poor governance (Agarwal, 2009; Altbach, 2009; Carnoy and Dossani, 2012; FYP, 2012). Despite recent efforts toward eliminating and streamlining some of the regulatory requirements, India's model for higher education governance is one of the world's most top-down, and most authority is exercised by the state (Enders, 2004; *The Economist*, 2005; Verbik and Jokivirta, 2005). Figure 1.1 presents a picture of the Indian higher education system. At the top is the Union Ministry of Human Resources Department (UMHRD). UMHRD is the primary national governing body. In addition to overseeing the National Universities, it sets policies related to quality that apply to all institutions nationally. The State Ministry of Human Resources Departments (SMHRDs) are state-level governing bodies that directly oversee the State Universities. They must all abide by the national quality polices set forth by the UMHRD. In turn, the State Universities each operate a system of Affiliated Institutions, which fall into three categories: public/aided colleges, private colleges, and autonomous colleges. Affiliated institutions account for the vast majority of enrollment

Figure 1.1
The Structure of the Indian Higher Education System

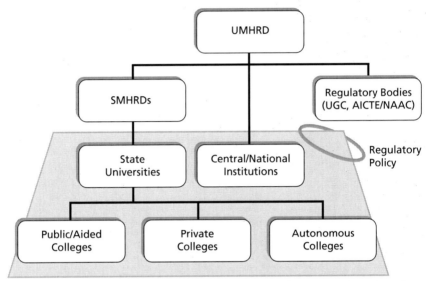

NOTE: UGC = University Grants Commission; AITCE = All India Council for Technical Education.

RAND RR225-1.1

(87 percent). Under the direct control of State Universities, these institutions have little autonomy over issues including curriculum, staffing, and programs offered (Agarwal, 2009). The SMHRDs also prescribe tuition fees and the quota systems that colleges must follow. Affiliating colleges thus remain something of an outsourced provider, with the state dictating decisionmaking across a broad range of areas. Some universities have hundreds of affiliating colleges across wide geographic regions, so the ability to carefully oversee quality is limited. Autonomous colleges are given more control over academic decisionmaking than other types of affiliating colleges, but still must follow the directives of the university to which they affiliate.

What authority institutions do have is also limited by a complex web of regulatory bodies at the institution, state, and national levels. At the institution and state levels, for instance, final examinations are set by a university-appointed independent body and must be graded externally. Tuition fees are usually capped, while teachers' salaries may also be subject to minimum wages as set by the state.

At the national level, while the UMHRD is responsible for setting and monitoring quality, its regulatory arms, such as the University Grants Commission (UGC) and the All India Council for Technical Education (AICTE), set and implement the quality standards that all institutions are expected to follow.[3] While these are usually harmonized with state-level regulations, the provider institutions must obtain the approval of the national regulators, which often leads to disagreements between the national and state regulators on jurisdiction (Carnoy and Dossani, 2012). This has led to a collection of unclear and often contradictory policies and laws that have prevented the government from implementing cohesive reforms (Hill and Chalaux, 2011). Finally, while the UGC is responsible for setting quality standards, India has begun to focus its efforts on developing a robust accreditation system, i.e., a system whereby institutions must demonstrate and maintain certain standards in exchange for endorsement by a respected, independent external body, in this case the NAAC. A National Board of Accreditation, promoted by the national regulator for technical education, the AICTE, also accredits technical programs.

Public Funding for Higher Education

Inadequate financial support from the government to meet growing demand for higher education has also been cited as a factor driving low levels of quality in the Indian higher education system. Responding to these concerns, the national government of India has increased public spending on higher education four-fold over the past five years and expects to continue the increases (FYP, 2012). States have followed suit, increasing higher education funding to more than 19 percent of total state spending on average (ASSOCHAM, 2010). India's higher

---

[3] These two institutions play somewhat different roles in regulation, with the UGC emerging mainly as a funding body, and the AICTE focusing on the approval of technical institutions.

education spending is now on par with many developing and developed countries as a percentage of gross domestic product, yet the growth has not been sufficient to keep up with ballooning enrollment numbers, and private spending has continued to outpace public spending (FYP, 2012; UNESCO, 2007). This has led to an increasing role for private funding in education through tuition fees, self-financing professional programs, and the establishment of new private institutions.

The allocation of funding for higher education also varies substantially according to institution type. A small number of national government institutions (approximately 221) receive more than half of national government funding. State institutions enroll 15 times as many students but receive relatively little national government funding and are underfunded by most state governments. The vast majority of private colleges are not able to receive any public funding (FYP, 2012). This has left many state colleges severely underfunded and most private colleges reliant solely on tuition fees. The private colleges are known to behave opportunistically to maximize fees, charging, when possible, auxiliary services fees, entry (capitation) fees, and other special fees (Agarwal, 2009). The increased fees have become a significant barrier to college access for students who are economically disadvantaged or otherwise credit-constrained (Herd et al., 2011; Hill and Chalaux, 2011). The national government's disproportionate support to a few national institutions has had two negative quality impacts. First, the funding gap raises the quality differential between institutions. Second, the incentive to raise quality is limited at all levels of institutions since funding does not follow initiatives to raise quality.

For those institutions that qualify for state support, the level of funding is determined by historical institutional deficits. Table 21.13 of the 12th Five-Year Plan, reproduced here as Table 1.1, shows the number of institutions that are supported by state and central government funding. The table shows the reliance on state government funding to meet operating expenses.

Funds are allocated by state grantors for specified expenditures, such as salaries and infrastructure improvements, rather than as a block grant usable at the institution's discretion. This provides incentives to run budget deficits and pay little attention to efficiencies in

Table 1.1
Number of Institutions Funded, by Source of Funds

Funding Responsibility	Universities	Colleges
National/central government—directly to institutions	152	69
National/central government— via UGC	144	6,285
State government	316	13,024
Self-funded	191	19,930

SOURCE: 12th Five-Year Plan of the Planning Commission of India, Table 21.13.

NOTE: The central government directly funds central institutions, such as the Indian Institutes of Technology. Grants for quality improvement and other support to other institutions are channeled through UGC.

spending. Accounting systems are often archaic, based on recording expenses against budgets with no use of accrual accounting or comparisons against efficiency standards, leading to inefficiencies in the use of funding (Jayadev and Ramesh, 2011).

Private institutions have incentives to cater to students in order to increase enrollment and bring in tuition funding, but in a market characterized until now by asymmetric information and excess demand, these institutions have had little incentive to invest in improvements in quality. According to Anandakrishnan (2004), only 25 percent of private institutions have transparent policies and aspire to provide a high-quality education, while the rest participate in "deceitful practices" and do not reinvest funds.

India has two main mechanisms to promote access to high-quality institutions for disadvantaged students: tiered tuition, whereby disadvantaged students pay lower fees than students who can afford to pay; and a student loan system that functions through the commercial banks with interest payments being tax-deductible (Hill and Chalaux, 2011). However, these loans have relatively low take-up, are not backed by the government, and the banks charge commercial interest rates and require collateral.[4] The Indian government is considering the introduc-

---

[4]   For more information, see the Reserve Bank of India, 2001.

tion of a large, zero- to low-interest student-loan program along the lines of that available in the United States.

The Purpose and Organization of This Report

As the above examples illustrate, the roles of various higher education stakeholders overlap substantially, and their agendas and the means by which they implement them often conflict. Recognizing these inefficiencies and sources of conflict, the 12th FYP calls for a paradigm shift of governance from a "command and control" model to one of "steering and evaluating." However, the 12th FYP is not intended to be an implementation document, so India now needs mechanisms for implementing the new style of governance. Policies that link quality and funding are increasingly used by countries as a means to create mechanisms to steer and evaluate a higher education system of autonomous, largely self-governing institutions. In this report, we describe how these policies are used internationally and how they might be adopted to shape higher education in India. The new mechanisms could play an important role in both incentivizing institutions to improve the quality of the education they offer and holding them accountable for doing so.

In Chapter Two, we describe the 12th FYP and the vision it presents for a new system of education governance. The 12th FYP offers a number of different reforms that can be used to improve the quality of the higher education system. However, it says relatively little about the role that policies linking quality and funding could play in achieving these reforms. To identify the range of policies that are being explored by other countries to link quality and funding, we present a review of the international literature in Chapter Three. In Chapter Four, we provide some recommendations on how these policies might be implemented in India.

CHAPTER TWO

India's 12th Five-Year Plan: A Paradigm Shift

In December 2012, India released its 12th FYP. The 12th FYP will be the nation's key policy document for higher education through 2017.[1] It highlights a number of challenges facing higher education in India and suggests reforms to address these challenges. A few of the reforms mentioned in the 12th FYP are already under way (e.g., streamlining national regulatory bodies), though most will be implemented over the next few years. To carry forward plans for increased expansion and to continue addressing issues of quality in the large and fragmented system, the 12th FYP calls for a shift in the governance of higher institutions away from the national government and toward the states and individual institutions. The push for greater autonomy among institutions conflicts with the web of contradictory regulations and policies that currently make up Indian higher education governance. The 12th FYP calls for a less intrusive role for the government and a number of initiatives to remove the barriers to self-governance. Rather than the "command and control" model of the past, the plan's authors argue that India should shift to a model in which the government role is to "steer and evaluate" (see Figure 2.1). The paradigm shift requires governance through greater accountability on the part of institutions, independent third-party validation, regulation by mandatory self-disclosures, and objective evaluation schemes.

---

[1] The 12th FYP provides policy recommendations for a variety of social services, including health, energy, and primary education. This report focuses specifically on the higher education component of the document.

Figure 2.1
The Paradigm Shift: From Command and Control to Steer and Evaluate

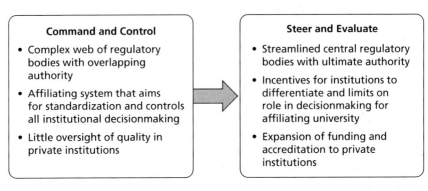

Command and Control

- Complex web of regulatory bodies with overlapping authority
- Affiliating system that aims for standardization and controls all institutional decisionmaking
- Little oversight of quality in private institutions

Steer and Evaluate

- Streamlined central regulatory bodies with ultimate authority
- Incentives for institutions to differentiate and limits on role in decisionmaking for affiliating university
- Expansion of funding and accreditation to private institutions

RAND *RR225-2.1*

New Governance and Stakeholder Roles

According to the 12th FYP, the paradigm shift requires new roles for the national government, state governments, and institutions. In summary terms, the 12th FYP proposes a move to less intrusive regulation by external agencies, more autonomy for the institutions that actually provide education rather than for the universities that they are affiliated with, a fragmentation of large university systems so that there are fewer colleges to be governed per university, and a consolidation of the large number of provider institutions into fewer, but larger and more educationally diverse, bodies. The 12th FYP also proposes to allocate large resources for upgrading faculty, for locating entry-level institutions closer to student populations, and for allowing the private sector access to public funds for teaching and research.

The 12th FYP and its predecessor plan reinforced the use of legislation to develop a new body, the National Commission of Higher Education and Research (NCHER), charged with quality assurance.[2] Other policy efforts strive to regulate deceptive practices, mandate

---

[2]   The future of the NCHER is in question given substantial concerns about the limitations that may be placed on state power under a strengthened central quality assurance body (Goswami, 2012).

accreditation for all institutions, and open the higher education market to foreign providers. The 12th FYP also challenges the UGC to shift toward policies that support the "steer and evaluate" model. One of these policies suggested in the 12th FYP include changes in the way institutions are funded. For example, institutions might eliminate detailed operational funding, in which they are granted money to pay for day-to-day operations on a cost-recovery basis, and move toward norm-based funding, a system in which funding is distributed equitably among institutions depending on their level of development. Other possibilities include shifting toward formula-based grants, in which institutions can anticipate how much finding they will get based on various quantifiable elements in a defined formula. Funds might also be awarded in a way that rewards innovation.

At the state level, the paradigm shift calls for states to set up councils for higher education. These state institutions would lead the development of the state's higher education system and play a guiding role in fostering sharing of resources among institutions, leading reforms, and supporting the research and evaluation of higher education.

At the institutional level, the paradigm shift argues for institutions to be categorized and oversight aligned with the goals of the institution. Institutions should be provided with greater autonomy, and the institutions should be incentivized to diversify (e.g., the introduction of community colleges, increased variation in purpose and curricula among teaching colleges, strengthening of research universities). The competition for students and competitive grants will provide external discipline to help govern the institutions.

Given the key role of the private sector as provider, the 12th FYP opens doors both to state funds being accessed by private providers through state-supported student loans and to institutional development. For instance, an ongoing World Bank program that provides funds to engineering colleges to improve their governance and education quality is being extended to private colleges for the first time beginning in 2013.

12th FYP Offers a Unique Opportunity to Improve Quality

The 12th FYP provides a unique opportunity for India to consider policies linking quality and funding as one mechanism for the state and national governments to elicit desired outcomes from autonomous institutions. In addition to the calls for greater autonomy and self-governance, the 12th FYP calls for increased funding for quality-focused efforts, such as greater allocation of research funds based on peer-reviews of quality, and increased *alignment* of quality and funding. However, there is no discussion of explicitly linking funding to quality measures as a means of incentivizing quality.

Three aspects of India's higher education system make it particularly suitable for adopting policies that link quality and funding. First is its size. Large systems with substantial private sectors are difficult to govern directly, and harnessing market forces to incentivize quality improvement offers a promising method for effective governance.

Second, because spending on higher education is growing, India has the opportunity to introduce quality-funding linkages through new funding opportunities, which should make the linkages more effective and possibly more acceptable to stakeholders. In contrast, many countries have faced challenges in developing and implementing quality-funding linkages because they have done so in times of shrinking budgets, with the primary purpose of the linkages being efficiency rather than quality improvement. This has resulted in a process that is more about stakeholder fighting over pieces of a shrinking pie rather than building strong incentives to improve and maintain quality, and governments have faced significant pressure from stakeholders to abandon the quality linkages (Carey and Aldeman, 2008; Salmi and Hauptman, 2006).

Third, there is a general consensus among stakeholders that India's current model for higher education governance is largely ineffective, suggesting that more significant reforms are necessary rather than incremental changes (Agarwal, 2009; Altbach, 2009; UGC, 2012). Toward that end, the fact that India has few existing policies linking quality and funding allows the policies to be designed in a way that aligns them with government goals for higher education rather than having to accommodate or modify existing structures. The design of a governance system based on policies linking quality and funding must be implemented in a cohesive fashion, with goals, measures, and incentives closely linked (Harnisch, 2011). Incremental changes to funding and quality can result in misalignment, gaps in coverage, and contradictory incentives. India's momentum toward dramatic governance reform provides an opportunity to learn from international experiences and strategically design a cohesive system that addresses the challenges other countries have faced.

CHAPTER THREE

International Experiences with Decentralized Governance and Policies That Link Funding of Higher Education with Quality

International trends in higher education mirror the trends in Indian higher education in many ways. The Organisation for Economic Co-operation and Development (OECD) (2008) identifies seven global trends in higher education:

- *Expansion*: Number of enrollees more than doubling between 1991 and 2004
- *Diversification of offerings*: Existence of many new institution types and delivery methods
- *Heterogeneity in student bodies*: Rise in access for women, older enrollees, individuals from minority racial/ethnic groups, and low-income individuals
- *New funding arrangements*: Diversification, targeting of resources, and increased student support systems
- *Increased focus on accountability and performance*: Growing focus on quality
- *New forms of governance*: Higher education increasingly approached from a management perspective
- *Global networking, mobility, and collaboration*: Increased internationalization (e.g., establishing branches of foreign institutions) and cross-institutional collaboration.

With pressure to support increasingly large and diverse higher education systems on budgets that are stretched thin, countries have begun to explore innovative options to move toward greater efficiency in spending. In developing countries, there are also concerns about fraud and corruption that have led to calls for greater accountability, particularly as governments move toward decentralized "hands off" governance (Salmi, 2009). This has led to a call for management-based approaches, with countries increasingly moving toward higher education systems that require strong accountability measures and clear links between quality and funding (Strehl, Reisinger, and Kalatschan, 2007). This chapter describes governance in other countries as well as some quality measures and funding mechanisms and a variety of approaches that other countries use to connect quality and funding.

Literature Review Strategy

Given that there is a vast literature on topics related to funding, quality measurement, and strategies for quality improvement, we limited the scope of the reviewed literature in two ways:

- Topic areas: We first started with higher education documents that had both "quality" and "funding" as major topic areas. We then reviewed documents that cited any of the following as major topic areas: "quality assurance," "quality measurement," "quality control," "quality monitoring," "accountability" and "quality," or "governance and quality."
- Countries: We focused on higher education documents that either took an international perspective or focused on the United States, China, the European Union (EU) countries, Canada, Russia, Brazil, South Africa, Japan, South Korea, Australia, or New Zealand.

The countries for the review were chosen based on the quality of higher education systems, size, and governance structure. However, with India's system of more 46,000 institutions in a federalized governance system with a complex web of regulatory and higher education governance roles and procedures, it is challenging to find countries that are a good comparison. Some of the countries chosen are quite different in size and structure, so we are cautious about making assumptions about the generalizability of findings. For example, the centralized governance structures of South Korea and many of the small EU countries are quite different from the federalized structure of India, so while in the small countries the central government often plays a focused, hands-on role in a small number of institutions, this is unlikely to be desirable or feasible for state universities in India. We focus on the high-level lessons learned from the international review rather than on the details of implementation, because the effective strategies of implementation are likely to differ substantially for India relative to these countries. Even the United States, with its federalized system of shared national and state control over a comparably large student population, differs from India in important ways, such as the existence of high-quality, nonprofit private institutions. We are therefore cautious in our application of international lessons learned to India.

After identifying the most commonly used approaches for measuring quality and linking quality to funding, we conducted smaller, more targeted literature searches related to these approaches. Priority was given to reports and articles that were produced by major international bodies (e.g., OECD, United Nations Educational, Scientific and Cultural Organization [UNESCO]) or were published in peer-reviewed journals. In addition to searching the literature, we visited the websites of higher education governing bodies to gather more information about policies and procedures related to quality assurance and improvement.

International Approaches to Governance, Stakeholder Roles, and Funding

To develop systems of self-governance by autonomous higher education institutions, governments and semi-governmental agencies continue to play key roles in governance, yet the nature of their roles change from direct oversight and control to monitoring and providing appropriate incentives to elicit desired outcomes. There are debates over the ideal place to locate quality assurance, whether it be within the government, under semi-governmental "buffer" agencies, or in independent or external organizations (Fielden, 2008). Countries that establish a Ministry of Education as the quality assurance agency provide particular clout to the ratings and the importance of quality monitoring. However, an independent institution for quality assurance has been shown to provide countries with a buffer against direct political involvement in the quality assurance process. Government control over quality assurance may also create the impression that it is focused exclusively on accountability, rather than supporting quality improvement. Reports by UNESCO and the World Bank find that quality rating agencies should be independent, either by establishing fully autonomous organizations or by ensuring a buffer between the government and the semi-autonomous rating agencies (UNESCO, 2008; Salmi, 2009).

The mechanisms for funding education vary widely across countries. A number of European countries have higher education systems that are primarily financed with public funding through the national government, while countries such as Brazil, Chile, and the United States rely on the private sector as a significant funding source for higher education. Federalized countries such as the United States, China, India, and Brazil also vary considerably in the share of funding provided by the federal government compared with state and provincial governments. Finally, countries vary in the degree to which tuition and endowments play a role in overall higher education funding.

An important consideration for countries is whether public funding levels and allocations should be determined within the government or by a semi-autonomous "buffer" agency. In countries such as Mexico, Chile, and South Africa, non-elected administrators and elected officials have considerable power in developing processes and procedures for funding allocation, while a small number of countries have established buffer agencies (Fielden, 2008). Examples of buffer agencies for higher education funding include the Higher Education Funding Council of England (HEFCE) and the Higher Education Council in Turkey (YOK). A World Bank review of higher education governance policies argues that control over the total size of higher education funding should be a political decision, while the allocation of funding should be carried out by a body that is free of political control (Fielden, 2008). This is a common method of funding across countries.

Another important question for countries is the role of the national government relative to the role of lower-level governments. Federalized countries such as the United States, Germany, and Brazil maintain strong roles for state governments in funding higher education. With the decentralization of higher education systems, many European governments have moved toward greater control of funding at the regional level, though the national governments retain a coordinating policy function. The United States has systems that tie funding and quality at both the federal and state levels. The national government provides competitive grant opportunities and requires institutions to be accredited to receive student financial aid, while the states have explored a range of performance-based funding systems to link quality with institutional funding. The level at which funding is provided and the responsibility for defining education goals and priorities are key considerations when determining the roles of different levels of government in systems that link quality and funding.

Determining how to address quality in institutions outside the traditional public university system is another challenge that countries face in building systems that link quality and funding. Polytechnics, institutes, and community colleges are more frequently put under direct supervision of a governmental authority than being integrated into the quality assurance systems developed for universities (Martin and Stella, 2007). However, some countries do integrate a broad set of institutions into the quality assurance system. The benefit of integrating all institutions into a single quality assurance system is that all institutions are held to the same standards, and the system is more transparent. However, if governments and institutions have different goals for different types of institutions, it may beneficial to allow metrics and standards to vary somewhat by institution type. In the United States, there is an effort to maintain similar quality standards by institution level, though there are in some cases distinct accreditation arms for four-year and two-year colleges (Martin and Stella, 2007).

With regard to funding, countries traditionally fund different types of institutions through different funding arms. New Zealand was one of the first countries to incorporate all institutions into a single funding system in 2002, and was soon followed by Ireland (Salmi and Hauptman, 2006). Similar to quality assurance, it may be beneficial to pull institutions into a single funding system to improve consistency and transparency, and to increase efficiency by eliminating overlap. However, integrating all institutions into a single funding system may reduce the flexibility and responsiveness of funding agencies to institutions with differing characteristics and needs.

Countries also must consider whether quality assurance and funding systems should include private institutions. In countries such as Malaysia, Singapore, and Hong Kong, quality assurance systems apply only to private institutions, while in other countries they apply to public institutions only (Martin and Stella, 2007). In what is argued to be the most equitable approach, Argentina, Chile, and Colombia apply similar criteria and rigor to the evaluation of quality in both private and public institutions (Fielden, 2008). With regard to funding, student financial aid offers the potential to extend public funding to private institutions. Voucher systems such as those piloted in Brazil and Colombia also give students more power to enroll in the institution of their choice (Salmi and Hauptman, 2006). The provision of public funds to private universities offers the potential for greater involvement of the government in monitoring private institutions for quality assurance and incentivizing the private universities through these funding mechanisms. Overall, the role of the state in the governance of private institutions will depend on the number and status of such institutions in the country (Fielden, 2008).

Considerations of administrative burdens are also important to account for in assigning stakeholder roles. As countries have shifted toward systems of autonomy and increased accountability, the administrative burden on institutions to comply with the accountability requirements has increased substantially. Universities in the United States, United Kingdom, and Australia have expressed concern about this significant administrative burden (Salmi and Hauptman, 2006; Salmi, 2009). In many countries there has been explicit resistance to the steering of institutions through increased accountability require-ments and direct links of funding and quality through performance-based funding systems (Aldeman and Carey, 2009; Strehl, Reisinger, and Kalatschan, 2007). However, recent trends indicate that institu-tions are starting to embrace the new paradigm of governance through accountability and are taking the initiative to lead efforts at increased accountability. Examples include Flemish universities that voluntarily joined a German ranking system, and the efforts of Australian institu-tions to develop their own set of indicators of higher education quality (Salmi, 2009). Many U.S. states are also beginning to take initiatives to lead accountability efforts (Aldeman and Carey, 2009). In addition to compliance with accountability requirements, the shift toward decen-tralized governance requires institutions to take a more active role in quality improvement through self-reflection and innovation.

One of the lesser-acknowledged stakeholder roles in higher edu-cation governance is the role of students and their families. In sys-tems of governance that rely on demand-based funding mechanisms to improve institutional quality through efforts to attract students (and their accompanying funding), students' choices of colleges play a key role in building the linkage between quality and funding. The com-petition for students in systems with substantial student-level fund-ing mechanisms tends to drive large numbers of institutions to pursue accreditation when accreditation is a requirement for funding (Martin and Stella, 2007). However, this linkage breaks down if students and their families are not able to identify or access institutions of sufficient quality. The government or other bodies must provide clear, transpar-ent data on institutional quality, and students and their parents must have the skills to use these data if quality is to be incentivized through tuition payments.

Measuring Quality in Higher Education Institutions Around the World

Measuring quality in higher education is inherently difficult, as col-leges aim to produce a wide range of benefits to students, employers, and society. These include producing productive workers capable of exceling in the labor force, producing research that has an impact on society, and producing citizens that actively engage in the society at large. Importantly, quality in higher education is inherently multidimensional. Institutions often have a range of goals, including providing students with the skills needed for the workforce, contributing to research and development, and developing an educated citizenry. For these reasons, most measures of college quality require a set of indicators, and these indicators may vary across institutions. In practice, the most quality measurement occurs either through institutional rankings, which include a number of performance indicators, or accreditation and other qualitative assessments of institutional quality.

Rankings or League Tables

The most commonly used method for evaluating quality in higher education is university rankings or "league tables," charts that compare institutions and rank them according to various measures of achievement. More than 35 countries have ranking systems (Salmi and Saroyan, 2007). These rankings rely almost exclusively on input measures, including incoming students' test scores, per-student funding, and teacher-to-student ratios. Of the 16 key measures used to compute *U.S. News and World Report* rankings, only two of them focus on outcomes: graduation rates and freshman retention rates. Concern about flaws in the methodology for rankings and the reliability of the measures led to 2007 boycotts by leading institutions in Canada and the United States of the respective ranking systems in each country (Salmi, 2009). In the United Kingdom, the Quality Assurance Agency (QAA) is particularly doubtful about the ability of league tables to provide meaningful quality measures, and recommended that this type of measurement system be avoided (McClaran, 2010).

Output-Based Measures

In recent years, many countries have moved toward collecting and publicizing a larger set of outcome measures that cover attainment, learning, satisfaction, employment, and research. The QAA considers graduate employability, rates of employment, salary, and types of jobs taken (McClaran, 2010). Other European countries tend to focus on research outcome measures, such as number of publications and number of Ph.D. graduates (Strehl, Reisinger, and Kalatschan, 2007). The United States has also been a leader in exploring outcome-based quality measures for higher education. Since 1990, when the Student-Right-to-Know and Campus Security acts mandated collection of graduation rates for first-time, full-time students, these graduation rates have become the most commonly used outcome measure. Many states collect extensive data beyond graduation, including test scores, employment outcomes, and student satisfaction (Aldeman and Carey, 2009).

A number of states have also explored the use of testing to measure student learning, including the Collegiate Learning Assessment (CLA), an exam that tests higher-order thinking skills, and the Collegiate Assessment of Academic Progress (CAAP). Measurement can be difficult and costly relative to measures that can be drawn from administrative data, but testing is attractive because it allows for more direct comparison across institutions and calculation of institutional value-added scores (which adjust institutional outcomes for inputs). Texas, for example, requires each of its state universities to administer the CLA to a sample of students in their freshman and junior years in order to provide a measure of value added (Aldeman and Carey, 2009). Eventually this may lead to full incorporation into the state's quality rating and accountability process. In 2009, the OECD announced a feasibility study of the possibility of measuring the learning of students in institutions around the world. The Assessment of Higher Education Learning Outcomes (AHELO) would be similar to the Program for International Student Assessment (PISA) in that it would measure student knowledge and skills, but the AHELO would provide results at the institutional rather than the national level.[1] However, there is skepticism among countries about the feasibility of this type of measure (Salmi, 2009).

---

[1]   For information on testing student and university performance globally, see OECD's AHELO web page (OECD, no date).

Several U.S. states are exploring the possibility of using employment measures, such as earnings, as a measure of the institution's quality (Cunha and Miller, 2012). Florida has been a leader in this area, tracking the number and percentage of graduates at each public university who are employed within the state, the number and percentage employed for an entire quarter, full quarter average earnings, and the number and percentage enrolled in further education (Carey and Aldeman, 2008). Student engagement surveys are also used to measure teaching quality and student engagement. In the U.S. state of Vermont, a searchable database of student responses to all of the questions on the National Survey of Student Engagement allows the public to review survey data at the institutional level, while Kentucky uses data from the survey to report on institutional rates of student involvement in community service, volunteering, and voting (Carey and Aldeman, 2008). Student survey results are also used regularly in Australia, Canada, and the United Kingdom (Salmi, 2009).

As higher education systems move increasingly toward output-based measures of quality, there are still questions about how to address the varying inputs that institutions are situated with, the goals they intend to reach, or both. Traditionally, this has been done through qualitative assessments of institutional quality that account for goals and inputs. However, in more quantitatively focused output-based measures, these differences must be accounted for directly. Some U.S. states address this by comparing an institution to a given set of "peer institutions" (Aldeman and Carey, 2009). In the performance contracts used by many European governments, the differences in goals for outcomes implicitly account for differences in expectations based on where institutions start (Strehl, Reisinger, and Kalatschan, 2007). Recently a number of prominent researchers were brought together to explore the possibility of calculating value-added measures in higher education (Clotfelter, 2012). According to the expert panel, these measures are not ready for use in high-stakes higher education decisions, but significant progress has been made toward identifying successful strategies to develop more comparable, outcome-based quality measures.

Accreditation

One of the most common forms of quality assessment occurs when an institution goes through the process of gaining and maintaining accreditation. Accreditation is used in Canada, Colombia, South Africa, and the United States, among others, and can occur at either the program or institutional level. The accreditation process typically consists of a self-evaluation by the institution, a study visit by a team of evaluators, and an examination by an accreditation committee (Vlasceanu, Grünberg, and Pârlea, 2004). Some countries evaluate quality "in relation to the institution's mission, which may include different standards for different institutions or programs, as established by the institution" (Eaton, 2012). Other countries evaluate institutions along a relatively standardized set of measures, with some small potential variation by institution type (Martin and Stella, 2007). The first strategy typically results in measures of institutional quality that are primarily qualitative, while the standards-based accreditation process structures qualitative judgments within a quantitative framework. The determination of how much to standardize the accreditation process and whether to base measures of quality on objective metrics must balance a range of competing interests, including the desire to encourage innovation and differentiation, the need to provide reliable information on quality to key stakeholders, the need to reduce the potential for fraud and corruption, and the desire to build trust in the system through transparency (Fielden, 2008; Martin and Stella, 2007).

Accreditation typically focuses on inputs and processes, including curricula, faculty, facilities, fiscal and administrative capacity, student support services, recruiting and admissions, and measures of program length and objectives (Eaton, 2012; Martin and Stella, 2007). These inputs and process measures can play an important role in measuring the impact of reforms to accountability systems, particularly in the early stages when it may be premature to expect substantial shifts in student and/or institutional outcomes. Many argue that accountability measures should eventually shift from these process-oriented measures of quality to output-based measures, as these are more aligned with the true goals of institutions to provide high-quality research, teaching, and learning (Salmi, 2009). However, movement toward output-based measures as the primary means of accountability does not eliminate the need for measuring processes and other types of inputs, particularly as countries move toward input-adjusted outcome measures. In addition to capturing early indicators of change in quality, these measures play an important role in identifying problematic areas and enablers of change and addressing barriers to quality improvement.

In addition, accreditation measures are typically one-level measures—institutions either pass or fail (Martin and Stella, 2007). The measure therefore provides no information about the range of quality across institutions that meet accreditation standards. However, some countries have developed measures with a range of possible ratings, such as the UK QAA's four ratings of "commended," "meets expectations," "requires improvement," and "does not meet expectations" (QAA, 2012). Indian accreditation systems are similar to the UK system. For example, the NAAC ranks institutions using an Institutional Cumulative Grade Point Average (I-CGPA) system. The I-CGPA can range between 0 and 4 points and result in a grade from A to D. A "D" grade results in a failure to receive accreditation, "C" is for "Satisfactory–Accredited," "B" is for "Good–Accredited," and "A" is for "Very Good–Accredited."

In many countries, there are substantial concerns about the fairness and transparency of the accreditation process (Hernes and Martin, 2008). This is partially driven by the qualitative nature of the accreditation process, which prevents the measures from being easily comparable across institutions. Countries that are concerned about the comparability and transparency of their accreditation measures can align qualitative judgments with quantitative values and explicit standards to provide a sense of greater objectivity (Martin and Stella, 2007). In some countries, there are more explicit efforts to prevent transparency in the accreditation process. U.S. accreditation agencies maintain a shroud of secrecy over accreditation reports, while universities in New Zealand and Pakistan recently pressured their respective governments to censor reports of quality measures (Salmi, 2009; Salmi and Saroyan, 2007).

Even in countries with well-developed accreditation systems, it can often be difficult to ensure widespread accreditation of institutions. The accreditation process is voluntary in most countries, and it is argued that the voluntary nature of accreditation is important to ensure a greater sense of responsibility for the feedback process and prevent institutions from trying to circumvent or "game" the accreditation process (Salmi, 2009). In order to encourage institutions to seek accreditation, there must be some kind of incentive tied to accreditation, such as access to additional funding opportunities (Martin and Stella, 2007). Status may also play a role in the initial stages. Colombia's accreditation system was one of the oldest in South America, yet relatively few institutions felt the need to participate. It was only when the country's biggest newspaper began printing the list of accredited universities that institutions felt obliged to participate for fear of being relegated to lower quality (Salmi, 2009). The U.S. accreditation system is widely considered successful for the high level of voluntary compliance, and this is largely due to the fact that institutions must secure accreditation in order to compete for a piece of the $227 billion budget for federal student financial aid. A World Bank working paper finds that accreditation is more successful when positive incentives are linked to accreditation rather than punitive measures (Salmi, 2009).

Policies That Require Institutions to Meet Quality Standards in Order to Receive Funding

There are many methods for linking quality with funding. They include government-based mechanisms, such as performance-based budgeting, performance contracts, formula-based funding (including formulas based on performance), and competitive grants. Other methods are targeted at students and include providing information to students that shifts their preferences toward high-quality institutions, and tying financial aid, vouchers, and other student-level funding to educational quality measures including rankings or accreditation.

Performance-Based Budgeting

One common mechanism for tying funding to quality measures is performance-based budgeting, in which institutions receive information on performance and are asked to develop budgets with an eye toward improving performance. It can be implemented through collaborative goal-setting or by simply informing institutions and expecting them to budget with consideration of performance weaknesses (Aldeman and Carey, 2009; Strehl, Reisinger, and Kalatschan, 2007). For institutions that want to improve quality but have difficulty determining how to go about it, performance-based budgeting can be an important tool to help them recognize their areas of weakness and understand how budgeting can be used to address these weaknesses. However, the performance budgeting process may not directly indicate to institutions what issues are leading to suboptimal performance and what is needed to improve quality. For certain institutions, the more direct role that quality considerations play in the budgeting process may incentivize institutions to seek out problem areas and make improvements. Alternatively, for institutions that do not prioritize quality, performance-based budgeting provides neither the carrot nor the stick for incentivizing them to change their priorities.

Performance Contracts
Performance contracts more explicitly tie funding to performance based on a variety of metrics on an institution-by-institution basis. Countries such as France, Austria, Spain, and Chile use performance contracts to ensure a commitment from institutions to fulfill a number of national objectives in exchange for access to additional funding (Salmi, 2009; Strehl, Reisinger, and Kalatschan, 2007). This allows governments and institutions to work together to identify common goals for improvement and standards across various measures. The flexibility of the contracts allows institutions to differentiate themselves and target various areas for improvement, while the explicit targets ensure a certain degree of transparency if the contracts are made public. However, these performance contracts can be administratively burdensome, and they are typically used in small countries with centralized higher education governance of a few public institutions (Strehl, Reisinger, and Kalatschan, 2007). Performance contracts do not necessarily mean greater transparency or comparability across institutions unless efforts are made toward standardization and clarity.

Formula-Based Funding (Including Performance-Based Funding)

Formula-based funding offers a more explicit way of creating linkages between funding and quality. The most simplistic and common form of formula-based funding is allocating funds on a per capita (or per student) basis, with variations by academic subject, mode of delivery (such as traditional classroom versus online courses), and grade level. The different sums are then aggregated and allocated in one payment, or block grant (Fielden, 2008). Moving beyond enrollment-based funding formulas, some European countries and U.S. states now include outcomes in their student funding formulas. For example, in the Netherlands, 50 percent of the teaching allocation is based on the number of degrees awarded, and in Norway, 25 percent of the funds are related to factors such as the student credits completed and the number of graduates (Fielden, 2008). By using outcomes rather than inputs, these formulas more closely align funding to the metrics that are aligned with the goals of higher education.

A more controversial method of linking quality and funding through formula-based funding is performance-based funding. In 1979, Tennessee became the first state in the United States to adopt performance funding for higher education. In its current format, public institutions can earn more than 5 percent in bonuses based on a formula that awards up to 40 points for student learning; 10 points for surveys of students, alumni, and employers; 20 points for achieving state priorities, and 15 points for learning assessment outcomes (Carey and Aldeman, 2008). Surveys of various stakeholders indicate that performance-based funding has been successful at increasing accountability in Norway, and there is evidence of success in a number of other European countries and U.S. states (Carey and Aldeman, 2008; Frolich, 2010; Strehl, Reisinger, and Kalatschan, 2007). Yet no country provides 100 percent of funding through performance-based funding, and schemes to establish performance-based funding systems are often met with internal resistance and the first areas considered for budget cuts. Countries that include performance-based funding in their higher education systems typically allocate 5 to 50 percent of higher education funding through these mechanisms (Carey and Aldeman, 2008; Fielden, 2008; Strehl, Reisinger, and Kalatschan, 2007).

There are a number of concerns about performance-based funding. It relies explicitly on the quality of the measure(s), so the difficulties with perfecting quality measures can diminish its value. Performance-based funding may exclude or de-emphasize key elements of quality that are left unmeasured, leaving institutions with little incentive to ensure quality in these areas. Small but valuable departments that had previously received cross-subsidization may be eliminated to focus on programs that bring in more money. The close ties of funding to particular measures may also pressure institutions to distort their missions in order to place exclusive focus on the measures attached to funding. Lastly, the instability of funding can be harmful to higher education. Given these concerns about the quality of the measures and the ability to link some aspects of quality without diminishing others, there has been great resistance to performance-based funding among administrations and academics who are used to dictating the institutional mission (Aldeman and Carey, 2009; Strehl, Reisinger, and Kalatschan, 2007; Fielden, 2008; Salmi and Hauptman, 2006).

Competitive Grants

Competitive grants are set amounts of money for which institutions, programs, and individuals compete. Competitive grants can be awarded for the development of new teaching methods or programs, and to encourage innovation in teaching and research, among many other things. Chile, Vietnam, a number of African governments, the U.S. federal government, and the higher education offices of some U.S. states have used competitive grants to encourage innovation (Saint, 2006; Aldeman and Carey, 2009). Funds typically are allocated through peer review of proposals for innovation, and eligibility requirements can ensure that institutions meet minimum standards in order to qualify (Saint, 2006). However, evidence suggests that if institutions are made to compete excessively for a limited number of small grants, as was the case in England, they will become frustrated with the competitive process, and the ability of the grants to incentivize quality will be dampened (Fielden, 2008). Individual grants for research can provide benefits to the academic field by increasing professionalism and allowing academics to pursue individual interests in research. Similar incentives could be used to provide funding for the development of high-quality teaching strategies among faculty in institutions that focus on teaching rather than research.

Incentives from Students and Their Families

Quality can also be linked to funding by providing highly accessible measures of quality to students and other members of the public that address information asymmetries and shift student preferences and enrollments toward high-quality institutions. Germany's Centre for Higher Education Development, for example, provides department-level data on a number of measures in an effort to assist international students coming to Germany. Rather than determining how quality should be measured, the website allows individuals to determine weights and aggregate indicators to develop individualized rankings (Agarwal, 2009). The state of Virginia has a stoplight color-coding system that clearly identifies how institutions are performing on 21 different measures. The Minnesota State Colleges and Universities System launched an online "Accountability Dashboard," with measures provided as automobile speedometer-style dials, each of which rotates along a 180-degree scale, from a "red zone" on the left indicating poor performance, through a more positive blue zone in the middle indicating "expected" performance, to a high-performing gold zone on the right (Carey and Aldeman, 2008).

Policies linking quality and funding through the enrollment choices of students and their families can be strengthened through financial aid, vouchers, and other student-level funding mechanisms that are tied to educational quality measures. For example, in the more than 60 countries that provide financial aid, it is often the case that minimal quality standards must be met through licensing and/or accreditation for institutions to receive the additional funding (Salmi, 2009). Similar requirements could be built in for per-student funding allocations and vouchers to restrict public funding from being directed to consistently low-performing institutions. In addition to setting minimum standards to qualify for funding, governments could tie the per-student funding rates to the quality ratings as a further means of linking quality and funding. However, while some countries (e.g.,

Qatar) have linked financial support through vouchers to accreditation for secondary schools, there are currently no countries other than the United States that require accreditation in order to receive financial aid funding.

CHAPTER FOUR

Implementing the 12th FYP's New Approach to Governance and Introducing Policies to Link Quality and Funding in India

Our review of other countries' experiences suggests some lessons learned to make note of, and potential actions to take, for the national government of India and other stakeholders should they choose to implement policies linking quality and funding as part of their movement toward "steer and evaluate" governance. We first discuss these lessons learned for India as it moves toward a system of more autonomous institutions. We then describe how policies linking quality and funding may be implemented in India, with seven potential policies for connecting funding and quality.

Lessons Learned from the International Review

Stakeholder Roles Will Need to Be Redefined

India's large, complex higher education system with its patchwork governance requires the engagement and interaction of a broad range of stakeholders to move toward the new paradigm of decentralized "self-governance" of autonomous institutions. If the pending bills for reform are adopted, the establishment of the new national agencies will strengthen the role of national regulators in defining and measuring quality, monitoring the provision of higher education, and shaping the landscape for research. These agencies will clarify the policies for quality assessment and quality assurance, research, institutional practices, and accreditation processes. The choice of quality measures and the establishment of market-based higher education systems that facilitate institutional self-governance will need to be enacted through policies that will require extensive debate among the broad group of stakeholders, coordinated by national regulators.

The national government should play a key role in the establishment of a student financial aid system. Student financial aid provides a means for financially supporting a broad range of public and private institutions while simultaneously facilitating access. This provides a unique opportunity for the national government to establish governance power over the full set of higher education institutions falling under the financial aid system. Access to student financial aid can act as a powerful motivator to compliance with national government policies for institutions, whether this involves accreditation requirements or other means of governing institutional quality. Given the importance of college choice in establishing the linkages between quality and funding through a financial aid system, the national government has an interest in improving the accessibility of reliable information on college quality to encourage students and their families to enroll in high-quality institutions and avoid low-quality institutions. The national government should play a key role in leading the planning for nationwide data systems, whether these data systems are housed at the state level, the national level, or within independent bodies.

States are the primary source for public funding to Indian higher education, so they must play a key role in any efforts to govern the higher education system through linkages between quality and funding. Regional governments exercise substantial control over state-level universities and their affiliated colleges in the current system, so the shift from "commanding" to "steering" will be most salient for these state-level stakeholders. As opposed to becoming involved with institution-level decisionmaking, state governments could build strong state-level agencies to oversee higher education, along the lines of the proposed State Councils of Higher Education found in the 12th FYP. While the national governing bodies would retain control over quality standards and many aspects of quality assurance, these bodies would be responsible for enacting regional planning strategies to address quality, access, and efficiency, including the establishment of new institutions, the development of key programs to fill gaps in workforce needs, and facilitating the collaboration of various institutions across the region. In addition, they would coordinate the standardized collection of key institutional data on inputs and outputs from institutions. State governments could retain responsibility for providing the majority of funding for state-level institutions, although funding strategies would shift.

Despite international experiences that suggest that accreditation systems are not always ideal for quality monitoring, the accreditation system in India could be designed to overcome many potential drawbacks and supplement other policies that link funding to quality. The active and voluntary participation of institutions in the accreditation system will also be essential to the functioning of the new governance system. Institutions in other countries that have moved toward policies linking funding to quality have noted substantial increased administrative burdens, and minimizing these burdens, or making them worth the while of institutions, will be key to gaining institutional buy-in. The transition to decentralized self-governance will also require institutions to retreat from the current system of affiliation and tight control through institutional standardization.

Colleges must be free to compete on their individual merits, and these institutions should be encouraged to differentiate and innovate to compete for funding through improved quality. But what if a college's experiments with differentiation and innovation fail to improve quality, despite its best efforts? After all, there is always some risk of failure that accompanies a new experiment. Since funding depends on performance, failed experiments might be costly, leading colleges to be wary of trying ideas with innovative potential. Hopefully, this will not deter future experimentation, since the promise of future funding remains to reward continued experimentation.

Students and their families are the final set of key stakeholders in an Indian system of governance based on linkages between quality and funding. As discussed throughout the report, students' college choices play an important role in establishing these linkages, and students must be empowered to choose institutions based on considerations of institutional quality to strengthen the incentivizing effect of demand-based funding mechanisms. To support their decisionmaking, students need increased access to reliable data on college quality, such as the U.S. Department of Education's new "College Navigator" website.[1] Through the proposed student financial-aid system, students will be financially empowered to choose institutions based on quality.

States, Institutions, and Other Stakeholders Will Need to Play a Larger Role

As the national and state governments transition to a more hands-off style of governance, the roles of these government bodies will shift. The state governments will have an increased role in planning for and promoting higher education policies to achieve state objectives. This requires states to develop an even greater capacity for strategic planning, program evaluation, project management, and budgeting (Dill, 2000; Saint, Hartnett, and Strassner, 2003; Patrinos and Ariasingam, 1997). The national government can help by providing states with funds and programs to develop their capacity for these endeavors, and by developing useful quality measures to help states determine how to prioritize funds (Dill, 2000). However, it is important to note that the impact of these reforms will initially be limited to the institutions that receive funding from the government, which make up only half of all institutions under the current system (see Table 1.1 in Chapter One). As the national and state governments begin to offer funding to private institutions through financial aid or other mechanisms, there will be increased opportunity to impact quality and funding by linking this funding to quality measures.

Institutions will have a stronger role in developing and implementing policies and programs to achieve their own missions and objectives. This requires institutions to develop the capacity for strategic planning, management, and budgeting (Dill, 2000; Saint, Hartnett, and Strassner, 2003; Patrinos and Ariasingam, 1997). Institutions are also the primary source of innovation under the decentralized model and

---

[1]   See U.S. Department of Education, Institute of Education Sciences, National Center for Education Statistics, no date.

will need to develop programs and policies to meet the demands of students, employers, and other stakeholders. The state and national governments can help by effectively communicating the goals of the reform; developing policies to provide effective incentives for institutions to achieve those goals and to innovate; providing support and training around new quality assurance policies, procedures, and tools; and developing and publishing clear measures of quality so that institutions can monitor their performance and students and families can use quality data to make choices (Dill, 2000; Saint, Hartnett, and Strassner, 2003; Patrinos and Ariasingam, 1997).

Students and their families have a responsibility to seek out and attend high-quality institutions and ask questions of the institutions they are considering. The national government can help by gathering appropriate data and making all information public. In addition, by linking financial aid to quality measures (e.g., accreditation requirements, varying reimbursement rates), the government can prevent public funds from going to low-quality institutions and incentivize students who depend on these funds to attend high-quality colleges.

Prioritize Defining and Measuring Quality

The first step in identifying the best measures of quality will be for key stakeholders, including the national government, state governments, and higher education institutions, to develop a set of goals for quality improvement (Miao, 2012). After identifying goals, stakeholders can discuss strategies for measuring quality accordingly. The specifics of quality measurement will require careful consideration of important priorities and concerns. There is currently no single acceptable measure or set of measures of higher education quality. The complex set of goals for higher education and difficulty measuring or accessing the desired outcomes often results in a limited set of measures that provide at best an incomplete picture of institutional quality. Because of the difficulty in measuring outcomes, most higher education quality measures focus disproportionately on "inputs" (e.g., teacher-student ratios, how much money is spent per student, and processes such as developing curricula). Those countries and states that do use outcome measures—graduation rates, test scores, etc.—face additional challenges with measuring these outcomes and accounting for inputs in their measurement. A challenge for the proposed NCHER will be to create a set of quality measures that will be dynamic and change toward more output-oriented measures as data become available, while still winning stakeholder acceptance.

Apply Quality Measures to All Public and Private Institutions

Given the large and growing role of private institutions in Indian higher education, it will be important for the quality assurance system to apply to both public and private institutions. This is also important given the call to increase funding to private institutions in the 12th FYP. Legislation in India—such as the Prohibition of Unfair Practices in Technical Educational Institutions, Medical Educational Institutions, and Universities Bill—will prevent private institutions from outright exploitation of students and their families, but full inclusion in the quality assurance system may be necessary to ensure that these institutions meet high standards for quality. Ensuring that both public and private institutions are covered by the accreditation is a first step toward system-wide accountability. Modifying accreditation to include more transparent measures will also play an important role in building trust in these measures and ensuring they are accessible to all stakeholders for use in decisionmaking.

Another consideration is whether training and technical institutions should be brought under the same quality assurance system as traditional colleges and universities. The current intentions are for the proposed NCHER to replace the existing regulatory bodies for higher education, including the University Grants Commission, the All India Council of Technical Education, and the National Council of Teacher Education. This would bring a broader group of higher education programs under a common quality assurance scheme, similar to what has been undertaken in New Zealand and Ireland in recent years. Alternatively, combining multiple regulators into a single regulatory body may reduce the ability of regulators to tailor regulations to specific types of institutions. In addition, a particular concern for India is the powerful role that this single body would have, giving states a lesser role in regulation.

Support Higher Education Quality in a Variety of Ways

We emphasize that policies linking quality and funding cannot be the only means of bringing quality improvement to a higher education system. While these policies can be flexibly applied to a range of goals for quality and a variety of funding sources, they are not sufficient to ensure a high-quality higher education system. A range of other supports may be necessary for policies linking quality and funding to be successful, including the supply of high-quality inputs (e.g., strong secondary schooling, high-quality faculty pipelines); means to learn about and share policies, tools, and processes that lead to quality improvement (e.g., effective instructional practices, quality curricula); the autonomy and resources to make the changes needed for quality improvement; and the strengthening of quality assurance bodies. Additionally, there may be some issues of quality in higher education that cannot be addressed with policies linking quality and funding, regardless of the supports that are put into place. For example, the lack of quality faculty is one of the major barriers for Indian institutions that aspire to provide high-quality education, but the pool of potential faculty in India is relatively fixed in the short term (Agarwal, 2009).

Make Greater Use of High-Quality Data

We discussed above how students and their families play a larger role in higher education systems that tie funding to quality as a means of governance. However, it is critical that the government ensure accessible data on higher education quality through broad dissemination and encourage students and their families to use data thoughtfully in making higher education choices. This will be particularly important as the government establishes a student financial aid system and other methods of funding that are tied to student enrollment (e.g., per-student formulas). The government and/or semi-governmental bodies should not only release accreditation ratings to the public, but also develop a publicly accessible system that allows students and their families to compare institutions along various measures of quality. Students and their families must also be taught how to use information resources to make rational college choices given cost and other student-level considerations.

Allow Time for Planning, Implementation, and Successful Outcomes
As experience in other countries has demonstrated, these policies will take time to implement effectively and may need to be adjusted over time to ensure that the incentives are effective (Maio, 2012). Countries at the forefront of incentivizing quality through funding are developing robust data systems that track students from high school, through the higher education system, and into the labor force. These systems enable calculation of value-added measures that account for inputs and are increasingly being made accessible to funders, institutions, and individuals. Yet even the United States, which is often considered a "success" in decentralized governance, continues to struggle with deficiencies in its policies linking quality and funding. Designing infallible incentive-based accountability systems continues to be a work in progress.

Given that India is not positioned to implement all components of a robust system of policies linking quality-funding immediately, it is important to consider how these components should be implemented gradually over time. For example, it would be unwise for India to implement performance-based funding before good quality measures are developed. Gradual movement toward policies linking quality and funding is also important to build buy-in among stakeholders. The government must think strategically about how to provide benefits to all stakeholders and frame developments in a way that does not alienate certain groups. Involving all stakeholders, including students, institutions, and state-level policymakers, in the design of these policies is critical to achieving this buy-in. That said, it is important to have a long-term view of the goals for reform, as decisions made in the immediate term can either facilitate or hinder movement toward a system that is partially supported by policies linking quality and funding.

Consider Other Education Issues in Addition to Quality
It is also important that the government consider other priorities in education as it moves toward a system of "steering and evaluating." Quality assurance is certainly an important priority for higher education systems, but considerations such as access, sustainability, and alignment with the K–12 system and needs of employers are equally

important. Policies that link quality and funding while serving multiple priorities should be pursued where possible. For example, a student financial aid system can facilitate access to higher education, while individual research grants can improve the academic profession, and institutional grants can incentivize collaboration and diversification. Ways in which quality-funding linkages undermine other priorities for higher education should also be considered. For example, a performance-based funding formula that is identical for all institutions could lead to even greater standardization and limit the ability of currently underfunded (and thus low-quality) institutions to work toward quality improvements.

A Course of Action for Improving Higher Education in India by Linking Funding to Quality

Based on our review of literature on international experiences with higher education governance, transitions toward decentralized governance, and policies linking funding to quality; our review of India's 12th FYP for higher education; and our knowledge of the unique context of Indian higher education, we make the following seven policy recommendations for India:

1. **Continue the Process of Developing and Implementing a Robust Accreditation System for Indian Institutions.** India has been moving toward a more expansive role for accreditation. In January 2013, the University Grants Commission (UGC), which is the primary national regulator of higher education, made accreditation mandatory for institutions that it regulates.[2] This stands in contrast to the literature, which suggests that voluntary accreditation with ties to incentives is more effective in driving institutional buy-in and compliance. In addition to concerns about compliance, it is not clear that existing accreditation

---

[2]   See http://www.ugc.ac.in/pdfnews/8541429_English.PDF, accessed May 22, 2013. UGC regulates all higher educational institutions except technical institutions. The regulators for these institutions are expected to follow UGC's lead. See edu-leaders.com, 2013.

bodies have the capacity to accredit all institutions. Yet India's accreditation system could be modified to overcome these and other potential drawbacks. For example, it could include tiered standards that are tied to the institution's own mission statements, shift the focus to output-based measures, and provide maximum transparency to stakeholders through broad dissemination of assessment reports. Shifts to output-based measures would likely increase focus on quantitative elements in the accreditation, and the effort to design a meaningful quality rating system would require substantial investment and standardization in the accreditation process. By developing policies that link financial incentives to accreditation, higher education systems can encourage institutions to seek accreditation voluntarily and provide accurate data (Salmi, 2009).

2. **Develop, Implement, and Publicize a Quantitative Data System to Measure Quality of Higher Education Institutions and Institute Policies for Continuous Improvement over Time.** A crucial link in the use of targeted funding as a method to steer and evaluate institutions in a decentralized system is a clear metric by which to gauge institutions' quality and their progress toward national goals. India should begin the process of developing and implementing a quantitative data system to support these processes. The first step is to engage stakeholders, including students, employers, government leaders, university administrators, and faculty, to determine the unique goals of higher education in India and determine a set of indicators to fairly and accurately measure institutional contributions toward those goals (Maio, 2012). These indicators should also adhere to basic best practices for high-quality metrics, including reliability and the ability to capture most critical aspects of institutional quality. Given the current state of India's education data system, the initial set of quality measures is likely to consist primarily of input measures. Over time as India improves its education data system, the quality measures should gradually shift from input measures to outcome and value-added measures (Clotfelter, 2012).

3. **Gradually Phase In Methods to Link Funding to Quality Measures.** The literature suggests that tying funding to quality measures can be a powerful tool to steer and evaluate institutions in a decentralized governance system. Our review of international experiences uncovers a number of methods to achieve these objectives, each with differing demands for the underlying quality measures. India does not yet have any national measures of higher education quality, and the current education data system places limitations on the types of quality measures that India can produce. India must thus necessarily start small and gradually phase in more concrete links between funding and quality as the education data system is improved and good quality measures are developed.[3] More specifically, India could follow these steps in developing and improving quality-funding linkages:

   a. Since India currently has no quantitative quality measures, initial efforts must build from qualitative assessments or easily collectible data. India could start by tying funding to the national accreditation process that is currently being implemented. India could also move toward funding institutions based on enrollment counts as opposed to a cost recovery basis. Institutions should, at minimum, be required to develop the data capacity to track student enrollment.

   b. As capacity at the institution and state level develops over time and India expands its education data system, India can transition some funding toward performance-based budgeting or performance contracts. These flexible methods to align funding with institutional goals have proven effective in many contexts, and can be implemented with varying

---

[3] While the strategies for implementing performance-based funding are laid out in this paper, sequencing their implementation is important, since some types of institutions may be more ready in terms of the quality of their reporting, orientation toward quality, and responsiveness to such funding than other types of institutions. For instance, the lower-tier state-owned colleges within state university systems are less ready in the above respects than research-oriented central institutions. The central institutions, given their already-established focus on quality, might be a natural starting point for these reforms.

degrees of quantitative data. However, this approach can be expensive and administratively burdensome, as institutions must work directly with the government to determine goals and develop methods to demonstrate progress toward them.

c. Over time, as India develops a robust education data system and a complete system of quality indicators based primarily on outcomes, some funding can be put toward explicit performance-based funding. This approach is less burdensome to institutions and governments, as the metrics by which funding is tied to quality are predefined. It is also often perceived as more fair than performance-based budgeting or performance contracts, which apply different standards to institutions as they set their own agendas in conjunction with the government. However, performance-based funding requires robust quality measures that assess institutions across all dimensions of institutional quality.

4. **Continue Efforts to Develop and Implement a Student Financial Aid System and Gradually Tie Eligibility to Accreditation and Quality Measures.** The 12th FYP calls for financial aid as a means to extend access to higher education to underserved populations and areas of the country, and that is the primary purpose of student financial aid systems worldwide (FYP, 2012; Johnstone, 2006). Yet student loan systems can play a valuable role in linking funding to quality by tying an institution's eligibility to receive student loan funds to basic quality standards. For example, the U.S. system ties eligibility to receive federal student aid funding to gaining accreditation, and the U.S. Department of Education is currently developing "Gainful Employment Regulations" that will require institutions to demonstrate that their graduates obtain jobs in their field of study and are able to repay their student loan debt at sufficient levels, as further conditions for participation in the student aid system. India could create similar accountability standards for its financial aid system to link quality and funding. This link will be strengthened as high-quality information on institutional qual-

ity is made accessible to students and families, who can use that information to choose higher-quality institutions.

5. **Continue Efforts to Expand Funding Available for Competitive Grants to Individual Researchers.** The 12th FYP calls for "more investment and focused efforts to build a vibrant research culture and strengthen the research capacity of the country," and increased access to individual research grants is proposed as a means to this end. Peer-reviewed research grants have been introduced and need to be widely extended to make most research grants competitive and open to both the public and private colleges, as is done by public and private organizations around the world. To increase the level of funding for these grants and align funding with the country's goals for higher education, the national government has established bodies such as the Science and Engineering Council of the Department of Science and Technology. The national priority-driven and peer-reviewed processes of such federally funded research bodies in the United States as the National Science Foundation and the National Institutes of Health offer a powerful model for these bodies in India. Funding for competitive grants could be used to create a vibrant environment for research innovation, as well as incentivizing innovation in teaching strategies.

6. **Develop a System to Provide Competitive Grants to States, Institutions, and Departments to Spur Innovation and Achieve Specific National and State Goals.** As opposed to student-level funding that is linked to general institutional quality, competitive institution- or department-level grants provide opportunities for the state and national governments to direct funding to specific goals that may change over time or differ across regions. For example, in underserved regions, states could use competitive application processes to identify organizations that have the best plan for developing any new institution. This will force organizations to carefully develop plans for quality assurance and continued quality improvement prior to building new institutions. These grants could similarly be used to incentivize differentiation, collaboration, structural changes

(e.g., merging of institutions), and a variety of other priorities that are mentioned in the 12th FYP. The World Bank–supported Technical Education Quality Improvement Programme (TEQIP) for technical institutions is already an example of such funding, and its success suggests there may be room to widen the size and scope of competitive funding. India may consider awarding these grants based on both the quality of the institution's proposal and the institution's general level of quality so that grants can be restricted to institutions that meet certain quality standards.

7. **Provide Funding to States and Institutions to Build Capacity for Self-Governance in the New "Steer and Evaluate" Model.** Some countries undergoing similar transitions have developed explicit technical assistance programs to help institutions and states change governance structures. Some countries have had success with academic audits, whereby institutions are coached by government officials through the planning and budgeting process (Dill, 2000; Saint, Hartnett, and Strassner, 2003). In India, the World Bank has funded TEQIP, which is designed to help technical institutions introduce governance structures that grant greater autonomy to institutions from state university systems on matters such as infrastructure and curriculum development.[4] If TEQIP is shown to be effective, it could serve as a template for nontechnical institutions and for widespread application to the private colleges as well. The specific approach for capacity building in India, if any, should be based on a clear needs assessment.

Concluding Thoughts

Indian higher education is at a transitional stage: The size of the system is growing rapidly, particularly among private institutions; government funding has increased substantially; and there is a call for a shift toward

---

[4] See All India Council for Technical Education, 2012.

a less centralized governance structure based on the "steer and evaluate" model. While the 12th FYP provides a range of possible reforms that are aligned with this objective, this report focuses on how the government will incentivize newly autonomous institutions to pursue outcomes aligned with national goals. Many countries with less centralized higher education governance structures have instituted policies linking funding to quality as a means to provide institutions and states with robust incentives to pursue national objectives.

In this report, we have reviewed the experiences of higher education systems across the globe that have instituted policies linking higher education funding and quality, and we distilled those experiences into a set of concrete lessons for Indian policymakers. Based on this review, we recommend that India consider using similar mechanisms to support the broad goals of the 12th FYP. Should Indian policymakers elect to do so, we recommend that India consider the course of action we've laid out to support the transition to a higher education system focused on "steering and evaluating" autonomous institutions.

References

Agarwal, P. (2009). *Envisioning the Future*. New Delhi, India: Sage Publications.

Aldeman, C., and K. Carey (2009). *Ready to Assemble: Grading State Higher Education Accountability Systems*. Washington, D.C.: Education Sector Reports.

All India Council for Technical Education (2012). Teqip. Web page. As of June 21, 2013:
http://www.aicte-india.org/teqip.htm

Altbach, P. G. (2009). "One-Third of the Globe: The Future of Higher Education in China and India." *Prospects,* 39: 11–31.

Anandakrishnan, M. (2004). *Higher Education in Regional Development: Some Key Pointers*. Indo-UK Collaboration on Higher Education—Policy Forum Workshop.

ASSOCHAM—*See* Associated Chambers of Commerce and Industry of India.

Associated Chambers of Commerce and Industry of India (2010). *Envisaging the Future of Higher Education in India*. New Delhi, India.

Béteille, A. (2005). "Universities as Public Institutions." *Economic and Political Weekly,* 40(31).

Carey, K., and C. Aldeman (2008). *Ready to Assemble: A Model State Higher Education Accountability System*. Washington, D.C.: Education Sector Reports.

Carnoy, M., and R. Dossani (2012). "Goals and Governance of Higher Education in India." *Higher Education*.

Clotfelter, C. T. (2012). *Measuring Colleges' Impact*. Context for Success Working Paper. As of June 21, 2013:
http://www.hcmstrategists.com/contextforsuccess/papers.html

Cunha, J. M., and T. Miller (2012). *Measuring Value-Added in Higher Education*. Context for Success Working Paper. As of June 21, 2013:
http://www.hcmstrategists.com/contextforsuccess/papers.html

Dill, D. (2000). "Capacity Building as an Instrument of Institutional Reform: Improving the Quality of Higher Education Through Academic Audits in the UK, New Zealand, Sweden, and Hong Kong." *Journal of Comparative Policy Analysis: Research and Practice*, 2: 211–234.

Eaton, J. (2012). *MOOCs and Accreditation: Focus on the Quality of "Direct-to-Students."* Education Council for Higher Education Accreditation.

The Economist (2005). *Survey of Higher Education.*

edu-leaders.com (2013, May 22). "'Super Regulator' NCHER Bill to Be Scrapped." As of June 21, 2013:
http://www.edu-leaders.com/content/%E2%80%9Csuper-regulator%E2%80%9D-ncher-bill-be-scrapped

Enders, J. (2004). "Higher Education, Internationalization, and the Nation-State: Recent Developments and Challenges to Governance Theory." *Higher Education,* 47: 361–382.

Fielden, J. (2008). *Global Trends in University Governance.* Working Paper Series, Washington, D.C.: The World Bank.

Frolich, N. (2011). "Multi-Layered Accountability: Performance-Based Funding of Universities." *Public Administration,* 89: 840–859.

FYP (2012). *12th Five Year Plan, 2012–2017.* Planning Commission. Delhi, India.

Goswami, U. A. (2012, December 14). "Parliamentary Committee Reviews Proposal to Set Up a Higher Education Regulator," *The Economic Times.* As of June 26, 2013:
http://articles.economictimes.indiatimes.com/2012-12-14/news/35819988_1_ncher-higher-education-regulatory-bodies

Harnisch, T. L. (2011). *Performance-Based Funding: A Re-Emerging Strategy in Public Higher Education Financing.* American Association of State Colleges and Universities. A Higher Education Policy Brief.

Herd, R., P. Conway, S. Hill, V. Koen, and T. Chalaux (2011). *Can India Achieve Double Digit Growth?* OECD Economics Department Working Papers, No. 883.

Hernes, G., and M. Martin (2008). *Accreditation and the Global Higher Education Market.* Policy Forum, UNESCO: International Institute for Educational Planning.

Hill, S., and T. Chalaux (2011). *Improving Access and Quality in the Indian Education System.* OECD Economics Department Working Papers, No. 885.

Jayadev, M., and G. Ramesh (2011). *University Finances (A Study of Karnataka State Universities).* Report to the Karnataka Knowledge Commission, Government of Karnataka, India.

Johnstone, D. B. (2006). *Financing Higher Education: Cost-Sharing in International Perspective*. Boston: Boston College Center for International Higher Education, and Rotterdam: Sense Publishers, 2006

Levy, D. C. (2006). "The Private Fit in the Higher Education Landscape." *International Handbook of Higher Education*, in J. F. Forest and Philip G. Altbach (eds.). Dodrecht, The Netherlands: Springer.

Martin, M., and A. Stella (2007). *External Quality Assurance in Higher Education: Making Choices*. Paris, UNESCO: International Institute for Educational Planning.

McClaran, A. (2010). "The Renewal of Quality Assurance in UK Higher Education." *Perspectives: Policy and Practice in Higher Education,* 14(4): 108–113.

Miao, K. (2012). "Performance Based Funding of Higher Education: A Detailed Look at Best Practices in 6 States." Center for American Progress.

NASSCOM (2005). *The IT Industry in India: Strategic Review 2005*. New Delhi, India.

NASSCOM-McKinsey (2005). *Extending India's Leadership of the Global IT and BPO Industries*. New Delhi, India.

OECD (2008). *Tertiary Education for the Knowledge Society*. OECD Thematic Review of Tertiary Education: Synthesis Report.

OECD (No date). "Testing Student and University Performance Globally: OECD's AHELO." Web page. As of June 21, 2013:
http://www.oecd.org/edu/skills-beyond-school/
testingstudentanduniversityperformanceglobalyoecdsahelo.htm

Patrinos, H., and D. Ariasingam (1997). *Decentralization of Education: Demand-Side Financing*. Washington, D.C.: The World Bank.

QAA—*See* Quality Assurance Agency.

Quality Assurance Agency (2012). *Institutional Review of Higher Education Institutions in England and Northern Ireland: A Handbook for Higher Education Providers*. Gloucester, England: The Quality Assurance Agency for Higher Education.

Reserve Bank of India. (2001, April 28). "Education Loan Scheme." As of June 21, 2013:
http://rbi.org.in/scripts/NotificationUser.aspx?Id=369&Mode=0

Saint, W. (2006). *Innovation Funds for Higher Education: A Users' Guide for World Bank Funded Projects*. Working Paper Series, Washington, D.C.: The World Bank.

Saint, W., T. Hartnett, and E. Strassner (2003). "Higher Education in Nigeria: A Status Report." *Higher Education Policy*, 16: 259–281.

Salmi, J. (2009). *The Growing Accountability Agenda in Tertiary Education: Progress or Mixed Blessing?* Working Paper Series, Washington, D.C.: The World Bank.

Salmi, J., and A. M. Hauptman (2006). *Innovations in Tertiary Education Financing: A Comparative Evaluation of Allocation Mechanisms.* Education Working Paper Series, Washington, D.C.: The World Bank.

Salmi, J., and A. Saroyan (2007). "League Tables as Policy Instruments: Uses and Misuses." *Journal of Higher Education Management and Policy,* 19(2): 31–68.

Strehl, F., S. Reisinger, and M. Kalatschan (2007). *Funding Systems and Their Effects on Higher Education Systems.* OECD Education Working Papers.

Sunder, S. (2010). *Higher Education Reforms in India.* New Haven, Conn.: Yale University.

UGC—*See* University Grants Commission.

University Grants Commission (2012). *Inclusive and Qualitative Expansion of Higher Education: 12th Five-Year Plan, 2012–17.* New Delhi, India.

UNESCO (2008). *Accreditation and the Global Higher Education Market,* Gudmund Hernes and Michaela Martin (eds). Policy Forum No. 20. Montreal, Canada.

UNESCO (2007). *Comparing Education Statistics Across the World.* Global Education Digest. Montreal, Canada.

U.S. Department of Education, Institute of Education Sciences, National Center for Education Statistics, "College Navigator," website, no date. As of June 21, 2013:
http://nces.ed.gov/collegenavigator/

Verbik, L., and L. Jokivirta (2005). "National Regulatory Approaches to Transnational Higher Education." *International Higher Education,* 41.

Vlasceanu, L., L. Grünberg, and Dan Pârlea (2004). *Quality Assurance and Accreditation: A Glossary of Basic Terms and Definitions.* Montreal, Canada: UNESCO.

World Bank (2008). *Global Economic Prospects: Technology Diffusion in the Developing World.* Washington, D.C.: The World Bank.